AF334733

Tallos de Luna / Moon Shoots

Tallos de luna / Moon Shoots
Elba Rosario Sánchez

Drawings by Robert Chiarito

Moving Parts Press

Moving Parts Press
220 Baldwin Street
Santa Cruz, California 95060
408 427-2271

ISBN 0-939952-12-2

Indice/Contents

Dialogue

let's peel away
all the layers
pull back the skin
reveal
our true insides
muscle and bone
liquid red
into a heart pouring
beating
let's peel away
breathe life
into our words
with the sweat
of our experience

Chicago

te pasas
los días
vaporizando

fuego hirviente
lamiendo
tu cara

una vez pensaste
que si había
un infierno

ya lo conocías
ahí viste
la muerte

se te acercó
casi tocándote
pegó un grito

el negro gordito
y se resbaló
cayó

tragándoselo
la olla hirviente
enfrente de todos

de hierro candente
se grabó
ese grito

dices que
te gusta
la palabra

steel
en inglés
acá   así es

infierno y también
steel
hielo

frío entumecedor
te espera
cuando sales a la noche

lluvia nevada
amenaza
congelando tu sonrisa

de repente ves la luna
y te preguntas
si será la misma

la misma
que brilla sobre
tu techo allá

abres la jaula
y tu corazón
vuela al sur

Cruzando fronteras

A mi mamá, quien esperaba las cartas de su 'viejito', quien trabajaba en Chicago

perseguida por tu ausencia
el pito del cartero
me hace correr
mis manos se adelantan
vuelan
extendiéndose como pista
para que sobre ellas
aterrice el sobre esperado
las conocidas letras

quizás haya una mancha
un hilo
un cabello
una foto
algo que me acerque
más a ti

al otro lado
sudas a chorros
te despiertan y acuestan
retorcijones
de entrañas
hambrientas

algunas mañanas
y muchas noches
te sientes morir
tan lejos de tu suelo
de tu gente

yo busco tu aliento
en esas cartas
quizás al desdoblar
las hojas
sentiré el calor
de tus manos

quizás
así llegue a mí
el olor de tu sudor
el sabor de tus palabras
risas besos
vía aérea
vía aérea
vía aérea

Crossing Borders

For my mother, waiting in México for letters from her 'viejito', who was working in Chicago

pursued by your absence
the mailman's whistle
makes me run
my hands advance
fly
extend themselves
like a runway
to land
the awaited envelope
the well known letters

perhaps there will be a stain
a thread
a hair
a photograph
something that will draw
me closer to you

on the other side
you drip with sweat
writhing hungry bowels
awaken
and put you to sleep

some mornings
and many nights
you feel yourself dying
so far from your soil
from your people

I search for your breath
in those letters
perhaps as I unfold
the paper
I might feel the warmth
of your hands

perhaps in that way
the smell of your sweat
the taste of your words
laughs kisses
will reach me
air mail
air mail
air mail

Códices

it was a time written
on the walls
in the belly
of the pyramids

      it was a life
      steeped in
      ancient rituals
      puffs of clouds

      from women's mouths
      wisdom of the clouds
      dance of the snakes
      yo ánima   life dancer

in the midst of the carnage
we resist
to hold onto
      the herbs
      the tobacco
      the sea shells
      the corn
our life's shields

it was a time
of Coatlicue
she giving birth
and birthing death
madre serpiente

it was a time when
stars fell
in a rainstorm
cornfields soaked
in blood
blessed plantas
de maíz
yerbas for healing
blood soaked
like their children

it was a time of the sun
screaming
it was a time of burning
scribed under our hair cells
imbedded under our skin
never to be forgotten

She-Wolf

This is
a hoowwwll
a she-wolf's howl
to steal the silence
a stone breaking
awakening
hoowwll

It is an echoing
that lingers
in the wind
restless
stirring in the night

this is the she-wolf in me
hoowwling
the night gypsy
masterful in her moves
sniffing the wind
ready to leap
and kiss the moon
hooowwwl

Lizard

here I am
contented lizard
I spend my days
belly to the sun
stretching out
without fearing
the dagger
of my imperfections
I am who I am

I awoke
from a long dream
ate the spiderwebs
that entangled
my eyelashes
blindfolding me

I do not eat
flies anymore
nor am I cold blooded
I am
my own midwife
showing off scales
of earthen copper
from head to tail
I give birth to myself

Lagartija

aquí me ves
lagartija contenta
me paso los días
panza al sol
cuerpo extendido
sin miedo
al filo
de mis imperfecciones
soy quien soy

desperté
de un largo sueño
me comí las telarañas
que antes me enredaban
las pestañas
vendándome los ojos

ahora ya no como
moscas
ni soy de sangre fría
yo misma
mi propia partera
luciendo escamas
de cobre terrenal
de cabeza a cola
me doy a luz

A Gift of Tongues

this tongue of mine
sets fires
licking hot
all in its path
scorches the old
announces the new

this tongue of mine
breaks through walls
setting free
imagery of feelings
odors of dreams
tasting the bitter
the rancid
quenching the thirst

this tongue of mine
invents the words
creating familiar signs
draws my days
in bold hues
celebrates
affirming
my world

this tongue of mine
opens wounds
heals the hurt
with warm breath
savors
the other
the you
that is me
this tongue of mine

Como golondrinas

entre las sábanas
de nuestras mañanas
se esconden
hirientes silencios
de este amor
golondrinas sin nido
agitadas
entre las sábanas
se buscan
se encuentran
y en un subir y bajar
de alas
vuelan
distanciándose
migrantes
para siempre

Like Swallows

between the sheets
of our mornings
hide
wounding silences
of this love
swallows without nests
they restlessly
stir between the sheets
search
find each other
and with a rise and fall
of their wings
fly
drift away
migrating
forever

Tepalcate a tepalcate

tepalcate (nahuatl : tepalcatl) fragmento de una pieza de barro quebrada

estos hombres
de ojos pálidos
llegaron un día
queriéndolo todo

nos forzaron
de nuestro lugar sagrado
nuestra naturaleza
sabia

donde hasta la más
chiquita yerba
tiene su lugar
su alma

nos arrojaron
a este frío hostil
pavimento de gris
mediocridad

donde miedo
nos tienen
y donde
nos hostigan

y aquí como en muchos
otros lugares

sólo rotos pedazos dispersados
les parecemos

de nuestra naturaleza
quisieron apartarnos
y nosotros de todos modos
pasamos de mano a mano

capas de ceniza
que entre huesos
piedras y caracoles
arraigamos

bajo nuestro techo
entre diente y lengua
vuela la pájara amparada
de nuestra naturaleza

somos tepalcates
de barro y física fuerza
que perdura en la montaña
en los barrios en la selva

tepalcate a tepalcate
nos reconocemos
somos caras en relieve
de una misma pieza

500 Years Now

they came one day
wanting everything
claiming everything
everyone

the land
the silver
the gold
were not enough

the blood
of hundreds
of thousands
was not enough

they wanted even our souls
familias died
dispersed
into four directions

we tucked
within our ear
the sacred beat
of our drum

embroidered
our songs

into the eyelids
of our blankets

500 years now
we have learned
to twist their words
round our tongues

to spit out
the poison of their privilege
their impositions
and inquisitions

500 years now
those before us
are here
we stomp our feet

dance in the palm
of earth's hand
our chorus of stories
tongues clacking fill the air

we
who are now
we
who are here to stay

Rumbamos

sacred is this dance
as sacred is the drum
communion of
hand and skin
        touch   touch   kiss   kiss
one pulse
one heart
two sticks beat the air
heat and rhythm
        that we thrill in
naked to our skins
        taca   taca   dun   dun
        taca   taca   dun   dun
hearts   in   a   gal   lop
syn
        co
                pa
                        ting
to this guaguancó
to this tumbao
to our of rumba love

Rumbamos

sagrada es esta danza
como sagrado el tambor
comunión de
mano a cuero
    toca   toca   besa   besa
un pulso
un corazón
    dos claves en el aire
    calor y ritmo
      que gozamos
    a cuerito encuerados
      taca taca dun dun
      taca taca dun dun
corazones   ga   lo   pan   tes
          sin
            co
              pan
                do

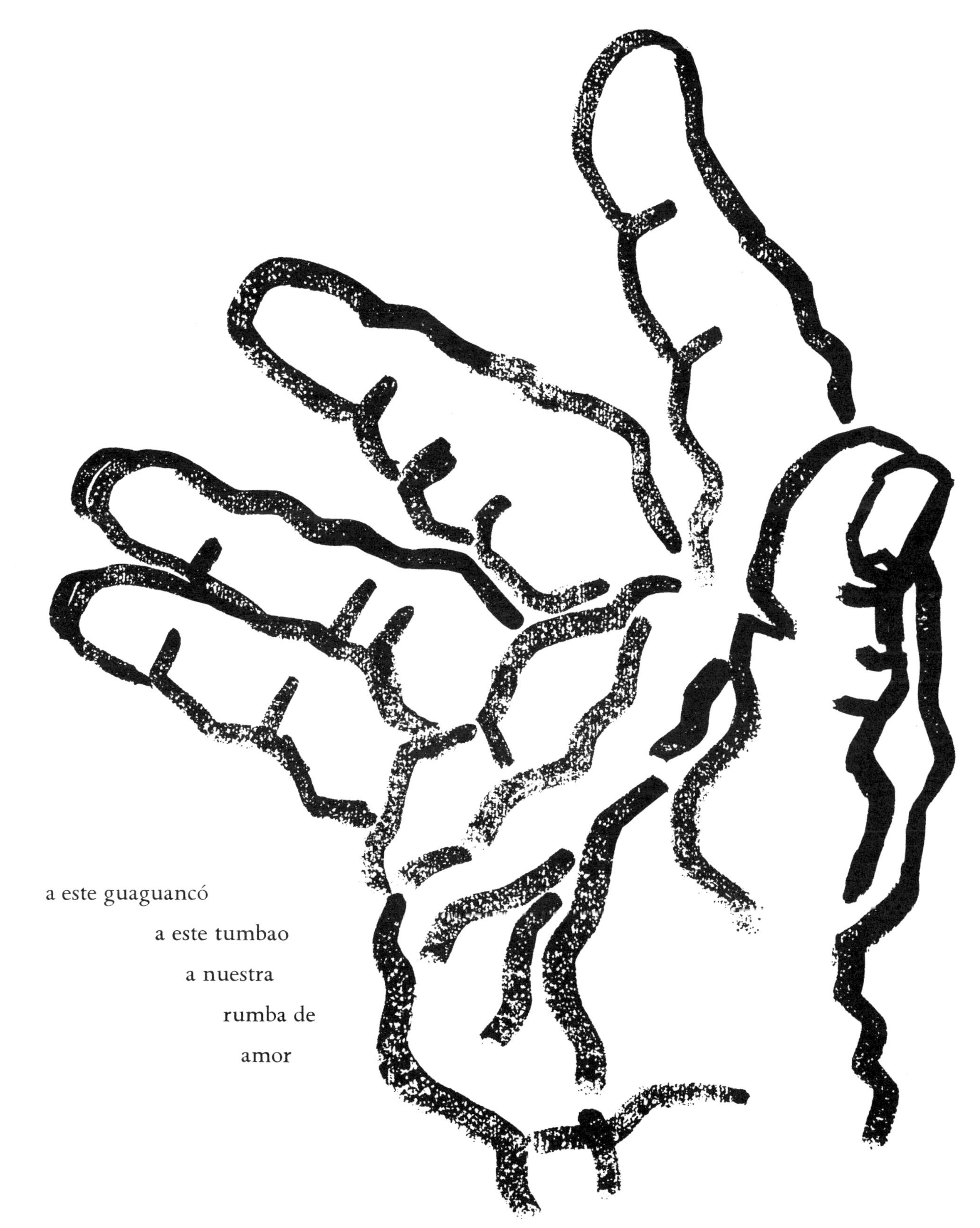
a este guaguancó
a este tumbao
a nuestra
rumba de
amor

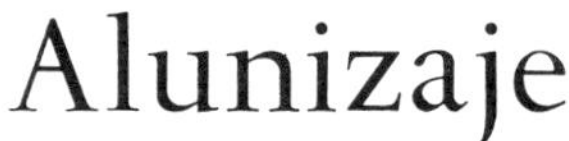

Alunizaje

para alunizar en mi corazón
necesitas a pie caminar
por arenas de futuras mañanas
sentir cráteres de tu naturaleza
empolvarte en cenizas
de huesos volcánicos

para alunizar en mi corazón
necesitas dormir en la almohada
de la verdad, vértigo y raíz
saludarle a este corazonalma
que acaricia las cuerdas de tu ternura
tú encendiendo mi esencia de luneza

para alunizar en mi corazón
de velos montaña azul
y rosas mexicanos
vístete
corazón rascacielos
pasión llamarada
te verás alunizando
en estos ojos
brazos
labios

Moon Coming Out

—mmmm mm m !
what's this
new thing
we've found?
I ask

from my mouth
a bridge
crosses our galaxies
I travel so far
I meet myself
again
in you

your long hair
trailing
your eyes
a flock of sparrows
your smile draws
wings
and spreads upon your
lips

you answer
    —it's new
       and
       we
       have
       found
       it

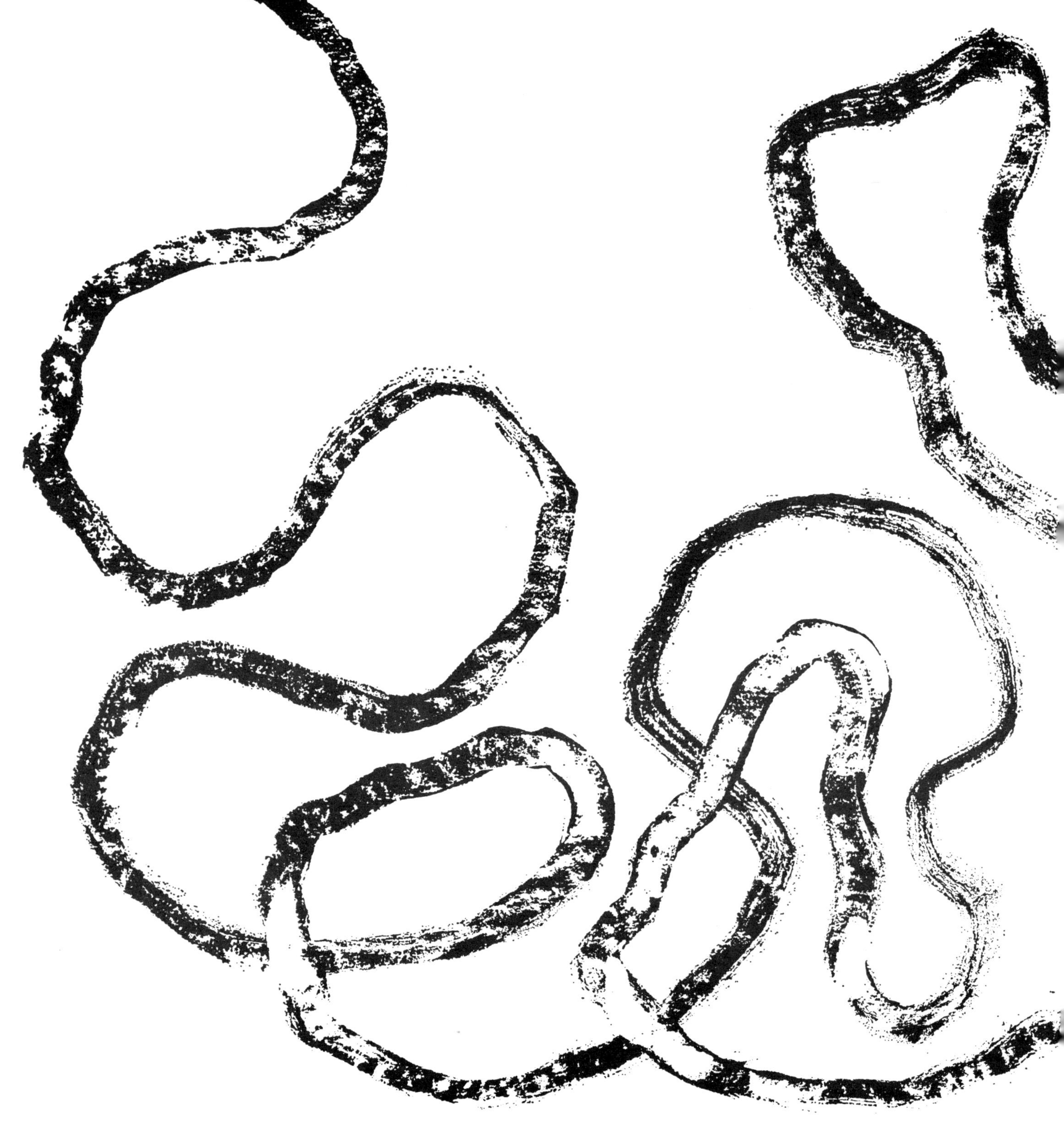

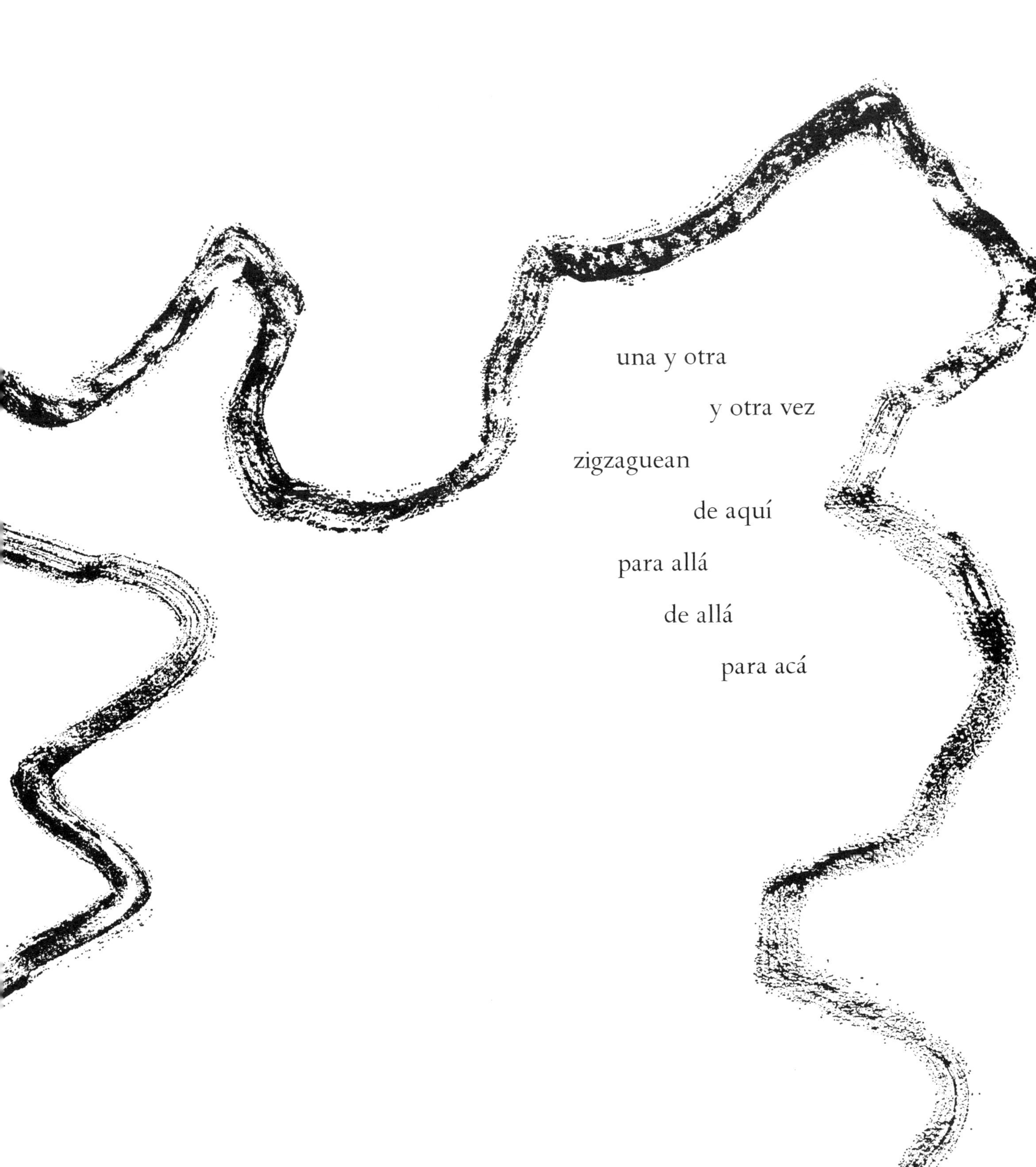
una y otra
y otra vez
zigzaguean
de aquí
para allá
de allá
para acá

<table>
<tr><td>

First Lesson

obsessions
are like snails
shell
swirling
each layer turning
into itself
again and again
      and again

zig zagging
      from here
to there
      from there
to here

leaving on our minds
transparent paths
sticky trails
that entangle
      slowly
entangle us
without end

</td><td>

Primera lección

las obsesiones
son caracoles
su cáscara
entornándose alrededor
de sí misma
una y otra
      y otra vez

zigzaguean
      de aquí
para allá
      de allá
para acá

dejando en nuestra mente
vereditas transparentes
huellas pegajosas
que nos enredan
      y enredan
lentamente
sin parar

</td></tr>
</table>

Astrohearts

what if

there were
no boundaries
our bodies
endless furrows
embracing
the heat of dawn
stars caught
in our mantle
of truth

what if

our hearts
knowing no borders
took a leap
into the unknown
and landed
ready to root
in lunar kissed
soil

Published in association with the University of California, Santa Cruz, *Tallos de luna/Moon Shoots* was designed and printed by Felicia Rice with Kathleen Biersteker, Michelle Blanchard, Elizabeth Chang, Dina Clark, Nysa Kline, Patrizio Pellouchoud, Ben Petty, Allison Prescott and Lyndon Ubana. An edition of seventy-five copies was handset in Spectrum types, printed on Rives BFK paper and bound by BookLab, Inc. in Iris book cloth and Moriki paper over boards: ISBN 0-939952-11-4. In addition, five hundred copies were printed offset at Community Printers and perfect bound: ISBN 0-939952-12-2. Copyright 1992 by Elba Rosario Sánchez. Funded in part by the California Arts Council and Porter College, UCSC.

ELBA ROSARIO SÁNCHEZ was born in Guadalajara, Mexico and grew up
in San Francisco's Mission District. Her work is included in the anthology,
New Chicana/Chicano Writing, published by the University of Arizona Press.
She is founding co-editor of *Revista Mujeres*, a bilingual publication for and
by Chicanas and Latinas. She teaches in the Spanish for Spanish Speakers
Program at the University of California, Santa Cruz.

ROBERT CHIARITO is a painter. In 1991 he was commissioned to paint
three large works for Oakland's City Center which are on permanent
display at the Cafe Fontebella. An exhibit of his work will be mounted at
the Museo Italo-Americano in San Francisco in 1993. He currently teaches
painting and drawing at Santa Clara University and the University of
California, Santa Cruz. He makes his home in Santa Cruz, California.

MOVING PARTS PRESS has published handsome and innovative books,
broadsides and prints for fifteen years. Book artist Felicia Rice issues editions
of new literature and contemporary art from her letterpress studio in
Santa Cruz. She teaches typography and fine bookmaking at the University
of California, Santa Cruz.